Remind Me

Juleigh Howard-Hobson

ANCIENT CYPRESS PRESS
Fort Lauderdale

"I should like to remain visible in this shape. The little of myself that pleases myself, I could wish to be accounted worth pleasing others."
—Leigh Hunt, 1823

Ancient Cypress Press
Fort Lauderdale
Florida, USA
www.ancientcypresspress.com

Copyright © 2013 Ancient Cypress Press

All rights reserved—no part of this book may be reproduced in any form without permission in writing from the publisher, except by a reviewer who wishes to quote brief passages in connection with a review in a magazine or newspaper.

ISBN: 978-0-9889648-4-6

Cover illustration by Mary Rae

Acknowledgments

Thanks to the judges and editors of the following presses, anthologies, magazines and contests, where poems in this volume have previously appeared:

14 by 14, Able Muse, Angle, Antiphon, Autumn Sky Poetry, Candelabrum, The Chimaera, Consequence Magazine, Contemporary Rhyme, Counter Currents, The Cycle of Nine (RavensHalla Arts), Enchanted Conversations, The Flea, Hawkandwhippoorwill, Holland Park Press, The HyperTexts, Into The Willows, LiverpoolPoem800, Lucid Rhythms, The Lyric, Mandragora (Scarlet Imprint), Message In A Bottle, Mezzo Cammin, The New Formalist, The New Verse News, The Pennsylvania Review, The Poets Guide To New Hampshire (NH Poetry Society), Poemeleon—TV Issue, The Poet's Touchstone, The Road Not Taken, Shatter Colour Literary Review, Shit Creek Review, Sommer and other poems (RavensHalla Arts) Soundzine, Soundzine, Spectral Lines Anthology of Contemporary Poetry (Nazar Look), Sweet Lemons 2: International Writings With A Sicilian Accent; Legas Sicilian Series Vol XIX (Legas), Tending Your Inner Garden Anthology (Golden Tree Communications), Third Wednesday, Trinacria, Umbrella Journal, VerseWeavers, and Wordgathering.

Contents

Remind Me   15

Do Not Look Back

Do Not Look Back   19
After the Fight   20
Just Once   21
After   22
ABIIT   23
Infadum Renovare Dolorem   24
The Girls in the Photo, Seal Beach 1952   25
What I Missed   26
ANZAC Day Service, 1938   27
To D E H   28
To Amber Who Died Young   29
Sooner or Later   30
Evening Clouds   31
9 AM, 45th Parallel   32
Twilight Reverie   33
Soon   34
Last Memory, With Dogs   35

What If

What if	39
Nerthus To The White Christ	40
The Burden of May	41
Hera Addresses Her Critics	42
Leda	43
Arthur in Mount Aetna	44
The Fair Wives	45
Embla	46

The Principles of Design

The Principles of Design	49
In The Spring	50
By The Way	52
Both Yes and No	53
Disorder	54
Quid Pro Quo	55
Small Things	56
I'll Have Nothing, Thank You	57
And Again	58
Elegy For Portland, Oregon	59
Work de Trop	60
Once	61
Touché	62
I Despise You	63

What Isn't Burned Must Rot

What Isn't Burned Must Rot 67
Branwell Bronte to His Sisters 68
And again and again and again 69
Apostrophe To Death 70
At St. Alban's Churchyard 71
Buttercups and Graves 72
Operation Freedom 73
After the Colliery Collapse 74
Ruined Cemetery 75
Winter Stand 76
Because 78
To A Long Dead Friend 79
After: Regarding The Little Mermaid 80
Don't Come Around 81
Respice Finem 82
To Be or Not To Be 83

Sparrows In January

Sparrows In January 87
Sonnenizio with Keat's Blue Sonnet 88
Nearly Still Life, Shire Morning 89
January Woods 90
Disting Fae 92
Vogelblut 93

The Grove In Shade and Light

The Grove in Shade and Light	97
The Sacred Spiral	98
Winter's Night, Farm Fields, Old Burton on Trent	99
Spring Softly Comes	100
Late Spring	101
Late April Storm	102
Winter Clouds: Liverpool	103
Unhappy Wisdom	105

As ever and always to Dave

Remind Me

Remind Me

Remind me to remember how
We used to feel, we used to be,
For I cannot recall right now
How you were you and I was me...
How we were young and life was good
And we thought that our every day
Would never end, and never could
Be out grown or cast away.

Do Not Look Back

Do Not Look Back

Do not look back. Listen: there is only
Sorrow there. All that we had, all that we
Made, all that we treasured, all that we were,
All that we thought would live on forever
And ever, are not here now. They're gone. Be
Saddened, be angry, be eternally
Robbed and broken (if that is what you are)
Do not look back
Though. No good can come of it. Sanity
Is all we might have left to wait and see
With, don't risk it wallowing. No future
Grows in yesterday's graves, so to be sure
That we'll have tomorrow, listen to me:

Do not look back.

After the Fight

Twilight is bruised looking tonight: pale sick
Yellow spreading from black-and-blue violets,
Green leaking out from slapped-face pinks. Huge, thick,
Clouds come and blot the last rays: the world gets
Duller and dimmer as the sky grows dark.
Now this evening's colors, the greens, the blues,
The busted-lip smears of red, the sallow stark
Yellows are all gone, have turned black. No hues,
No shades, no interplay of tones. Just black
That admits no moon and allows no stars
Because it is blackness made from a lack
Of light, cloud hung, absolute. Abattoir
Dark, mausoleum dark, a painful dark
That reminds me how unhealed bruises mark.

Just Once

Just once to see that I meant more—
A glimpse, perhaps—a shadow's grey—
Than all the rest who've gone before
And all so quickly gone away…

Just to know that I exacted
More than a brief and blurry time—
More than a pale and weak enactment…
To know your pain's as deep as mine.

After

The great art of life is sensation,
to feel that we exist, even in pain.
—Byron

If we should ever talk again
Now, after all these damning years...
Should we need to stop and explain
That time of silence? Or refrain
From explanations? It's not clear,
(If we should ever talk again),
What we would do, for we contain
Too many memories, my dear.
Should we need to stop and explain
Each and every one of them? Pain
Or no pain—what would we most fear
If we should ever talk again?
I think I'd fear no pain. Disdain
Or even hate would be less severe
Should we need to stop and explain
Anything. So let us abstain
From the conceit to be sincere
If we should ever talk again...
Should we need to stop and explain.

ABIIT
for Dave

I cannot think of when time will
Come here upon us certainly;
The day I wake when you are still
And you do not answer me.
I cannot bear to think of you
Cold and dead—passed to unknown—
Alone and lost. What will you do?
How could I leave you, dead, alone?
How could I leave you to that night
That falls upon the hapless dead?
To hope and pray you are alright,
And hope and pray there is no dread:
That you don't cry, that you don't weep,
That you are not alone and far
Away somewhere. Hope that you sleep
And wake in peace. And that you are
Somehow still you, and fine, and warm.
With hope, with light, with company;
No fear, no cold, no dark alarm;
Just waiting patiently for me.

Infadum Renovare Dolorem

We never thought our youth would pass.
We were the clever ones, the new,
The young, the cool, the smart, the fast.
We had so many things to do.

But, somehow, nothing much got done.
Our days and weeks of youth went on
And on, and somehow everyone
Got older.
   And our days were done.

The Girl in the Photo, Seal Beach 1952

Yes. I resent you for looking so young—
All pale, smooth skin and perfect muscle tone;
Your faded photograph face still seems so
Beautiful, even now. But me? I'm hung
In withered skin and graying hair. A crone –
Grown baggy, hideous, over-aged. No
More lovely long limbed boys ever look at
Me these days. It's not fair that you kept your
Slender beauty while I fell apart. I
Hate you for your youthfulness and all that
This old image pretends to be. Before,
We both were lovely girls. I didn't die
Like you did, though. I aged, as women will,
While you...you drowned...and remain lovely still.

What I Missed
for Josephine Howard, 1916-1998

I came to visit you in '86.
I was twenty four, mad for Lambrettas
And the boys who rode them. You showed me tricks
Your cat could do, that first evening, sweater
Half knitted and hanging from your knees, tea
On the boil in the kitchen. I smiled, made
My break for it the next morning. Watford
Wasn't where it was at, for me. I stayed
With you just long enough to be nice, bored
Inside and out with your old company,
Your garden and your memories of war...
I thought myself too clever to want you
Instead of London. I was twenty four.
I'm older now and wish I'd wanted to.

ANZAC Day Service, 1938

"They shall not grow old as we who are left
Grow old", they say. I stop and think: perhaps
They do. What else would they do in the gaps
Between back then and now? Within that cleft
Of years? Of course they have grown old—and I
Am glad for it, for so have I. Old frames
Surround old photographs, signed by old names
So long ago—all things grow old. You died
Too soon, perhaps, to age and wither gray
In people's memories, not like you'd been
Here with us through all these years...But, again,
You must grow old with me because today
I am grown old and you and I were one.
You can't stay young now all my youth is done.

To D E H

I cannot bear that we must die
That one day, someday, time will come
And Death shall sever you and I.
Death shall beat his muffled drum
Death shall shriek his piercing cry
Death shall leave us—two. Not one.

To Amber Who Died Young

And when we stop to think of you
We find you now so far behind—
We did not know how much we'd mind
The space that marks times old and new.

The space that marks you dead and gone,
We didn't know it never ends,
We didn't plan on other friends
Filling in where we went on.

Where we went on, and you did not.
We have changed so much since then.
It all has changed so much since when
You died. It seems we all forgot

That life moves on, and people leave
Old times to fade and fall away,
No matter what they used to say,
No matter what we all believe.

Sooner or Later

It will come, the end of me, by and by,
That wretched day when all I am is gone.
Old age, madness, anger they'll have their try
And what they don't get, death will happen on.

All of it—the little bits that make our
Time here seem as if it were worth the while,
As well as the bigger things like power,
Love, success—will fade away. Denial

Won't stop it, acceptance won't help. It just
Will come, and then I shall no longer be
Myself. Only ashes to ashes, dust
To dust, me to nothing left of me.

Evening Clouds

Cloud upon more cloud, white on shades of white,
Grey or bloody backed in the setting sun
They pile, each touching each, as the twilight
Down fades, pulling back ruddy tendrils—one
By one, in long streaks—until all are gone.
The sky turns dark. The last of day turns night.
No stars appear. No moon. But branches, black
Against the mass of cloud, are slowly shown,
Stark and skeletonly. Across, then back,
They weave among themselves, each one alone
One minute, enmeshed the next: tree tops blown
Then blown again by winds. Leafless limbs crack
And groan beneath the moonless, starless, sky,
While over them the clouds sit darkly by.

9 AM, 45th Parallel

Smoke rises from the roof [not ash but steam],
Up-wisping before blowing out across
The yard. The damp leafless trees make it seem
Still winter despite it being spring. Moss
And stone lend to the general feeling
Of this permanent gloom, each just a dim
Grey in the morning's light. Shadows, stealing
Between the bare cold branches, become grim
Within the murky confines of the mist
Still rising and still falling down upon
The chilly ground. No sunlight ever sifts
Through the shade darkened places to bring some
Relief to the seemingly endless grays.
They just collect—and chase all light away.

Twilight Reverie

Here, sitting here, in the half dark, with the
bush beans and the pumpkin vines and fennel
that is just beginning to bloom with a
lacy blur of greenish yellow, pell mell
and bright in the grey air of dusk while beet
leaves, scarlet shot and earwig bitten, catch
the eye beneath a strand of bittersweet
nightshade, (the only vile weed in the patch
but what lovely violet blossoms and blood
red berries), as the shadows climb across
the rows and meet the fence...
I've understood
little of how a garden grows; I toss
seeds in holes, give them water, uproot weeds
and somehow, some how, life itself proceeds.

Soon

We sit and wait for time to tell,
For fortune's kiss to bless the bold—
Creating heavens out of hell
While we grow old...
we just grow old...

Last Memory, With Dogs

When I was younger—I'd just turned nineteen—
I went for a last walk with my old man.
We took two dogs of his along, being
A convenient excuse to have at hand
For what we were both doing (it wasn't
A close relationship, mine and my dad's).
Neither of us spoke until, as we went
West, we saw the sun setting. I had
Never cared about sunsets before, but
The sudden scarlet beauty of the sky,
(Plus his dying), made me say: "Look." "Know what
Makes the light look red like that?" he coughed. I
Said: "No." He spat. "Pollution." We turned back,
The dogs tired, their leashes hanging slack.

What If

What If

And what if, in fact, he already came
Again, that once and future king of ours
But we didn't recognize him? No shame
In that, of course, how could we know? Arthur's
A common enough name. And, he
Might have appeared, but named as someone else,
When we were pre-occupied. Wars. Plagues. We
Couldn't predict when his rebirth should've
Occurred—or which exact emergency
Would summon him. Do we believe enough
In our myths, in our tales about our son
Of suns, of ages long foretold and of
Ages promised...and did we miss the one
Who managed to arrive here once-upon?

Nerthus to the White Christ
(regarding the loaves and fishes thing)

You've really swayed the crowds with this—
You up-start vegetation god.
There was a time they'd call it odd
That any born of earth, of clod,
Should try to claim their souls as his.

There was a time—a while ago—
You were, in their minds and hearts,
Some foreign god, designed for parts
When winter ends and spring time starts—
But now, they don't consign you so.

For, now, you've got the masses where
Once I ruled in caves and woods—
Where once my statues proudly stood,
There's only you these days. You should
Be happy...and you should beware.

The Burden of May

And so it is that it is over, all
Of our brightness dimmed, our visions damned. End
Without end now. It is impossible
To think everything we loved is gone when
We survive...Surely this is a nightmare,
We will wake, all of us, and it will be
Mid April, not May, we'll be anywhere
But here, at the end of it all. But we
Know, deep in our hearts, we cannot do that
Because we are not asleep, it is May,
And we're alive. Our burden, then, is what
To do now, what to live for now. Today
It is May and we must continue from
Here if a new April should ever come.

Hera Addresses Her Critics
(an ovillejo—'tangled ball of yarn')

Peas, old copper, mint, the leprechaun,
Frog spawn,
Various fungi, mosses, peacocks,
Flower stalks,
Emeralds, some apples, most leaves, the sea.
Not me,
Though you'd love to think it. Envy
Is something I don't need.
Some things are green, agreed—
Frog spawn, flower stalks—not me.

Leda

I am air, I am earth, feather, flesh, sky,
Flower, bird. I am all of these. Grey, white,
Pink, orange, blue surround me. I
Dance within, below, above, behind. Night
Frames my movements as we swirl, my fine swans
And I, blending into sacred spirals,
Blending into sacred dance. Fleet wings, bronze
Braids, pink skin, bright eyes—each one of us rolls
Into the other, around and around
We go, while darkness watches without star
Or moon to distract it from our profound
Madrigals. I am Leda, am Ishtar,
Am Valkyrie. I am all and more than
All. I am life, dance, spiral, goddess, swan.

Arthur In Mount Aetna

As strange as it may seem for an English King to
sleep in a Sicilian Cavern, many legends have been
told of King Arthur sleeping—accompanied with his
Guardian Knights and horses—in a hidden cave in
the hills of Mount Aetna, where he must remain until
his wounds heal. Once they are healed, he can return
to his native land to fulfill his destiny as the Once
and Future King, the savior of England in her time of need.

My fatal wound runs fresh each dawning day—
So, we sleep on within this place. My knights,
My horses each rest around me. Away,
Far away, from what we call home. Old plights
Such as ours, though, seem real no longer to
The current world. No matter, we remain
Here sleeping still. We'll keep our slumber through
The long black nights, and longer days again,
That come and pass. One day our dreaming hearts
Will loose these sleeping bonds and wake. It is
Important that I rest 'til then, in parts
Of Aetna's hills where none seek, for once this
Foul wound of mine is healed, we wake—and must
Return to England: England will need us.

The Fair Wives

There's always talk of the knights, hidden deep
Within their mountains. Waiting waiting for
The right time, the right day, to shake off sleep
And save the world from danger. The folklore
Never makes mention of us, the fair wives,
And yet, we lie here hidden just as far
And deep as any armoured man. Our lives
Are similarly suspended. We are
Entombed within these craggy caves, bid to
Wait, silently and unremarkedly,
Until the right time comes for us to do
What we wait for: rouse this sleeping medley
Of knights who dream, and send them forth from here
To save the world and all that we hold dear.

Embla

I have no interest in your arches and
Your bells, your phallic spires that do not
Inspire so much as they intrude. Land
And sky was not intended to be what
Men build such interruptions on. I do
Not want to look North and see your slanted
Roofline and your cross before my eyes, to
Know that you have had your way, have planted
Your saints and your sinners in my world, that
Your stained windows corrupt my holy sun,
That your prayers tear my sacred vril. Hallstatt,
Stonehenge, Boleigh: deserted, defiled, done,
Their pagan souls attacked by your dark gods
Who came with words of love, but stayed at odds.

The Principles of Design

The Principles of Design

Don't tell me there isn't any pattern.
It can be seen over and over. Here
It is: divide and conquer, us and them,
Left and right. An agenda based on fear
Of who the others are, could be, might do…
Creating dread that everything could crash
If its own system is not stretched—here to
There—to shield the modern world from the rash
Interests of that post-modern other (which
Has no interest in the universal,
Does not like the status quo, is not rich
From global loans, and does not care, at all,
About you). The pattern's clear: it connects
Those dots of doubts it makes while it protects.

In the Spring

The old stump sits, heavy barked, with fat roots
That ride up from the ground like some long backed
School of serpents. Where it's been chopped, thin shoots
With shiny skins rise up: thin fingers, tacked
Upon a mighty hand, that sway and end
Among their own selves. Everywhere on them
Are small blooms, tiny leaves. Far under them
The curtailed tree soaks up water through roots
That once fed a giant. Now that thirst must end
In sips that gently flow to flowers backed
Not by huge branches but slight sticks grown tacked,
Rangy, struggling to stay alive. Shoots

All the more fragile because they are shoots
Not shot from seed but from a stump. It's them
Or nothing, though. Fragile or not, each tacked
Twig is a final gasp and these thick roots
Know. Once there was an orchard this tree backed.
An orchard that ran all along the end
Of the ridge to the river. The far end
Was a pasture. And every year shoots
Of new trees grew up from last years fruit. Backed
By meadow and water, each one of them
Had time to flower and to put down roots
Before they were sold, using small signs tacked

On rail fences: "Fruit trees for sale", or tacked
Up in feed stores. That was before the end
Of orchards and farms around here. The roots
Of that life are dug up. A highway shoots
Though where the old farm roads were. All of them,
All the farms, all the old places that backed
Their fields to each other. Gone. None were backed

By money for higher taxes when—tacked
Along the highways—came progress. To them,
Of course, it wasn't progress. It meant "end":
Their end. New developments, not new shoots,
Would sprout in their meadows, disturbing roots.

This land's backed up with houses, end to end,
Each tacked to a yard where old stumps send shoots
In spring, fed by roots still attached to them.

By The Way

Oh my god I saw him, he looked to be
A million. He looked so badly broken,
So motionless and silent. Please tell me
What happened. He used to be well spoken
Of when the party was in favor. I
Don't recall the reason, or if there
Even was one, for him being any
Sort of target. I was not made aware
Of his being some one hated, more than
Any one like him is hated. Was he
Gaining ground too quickly? Had he begun
Learning secrets? They broke him completely,
How bad he must have suffered. I hope they
Know we two weren't close friends, by the way.

Both Yes and No

Both yes and no is all I have to say:
Yes, I love you. No, I don't. Yes and no,
Depending on the timing of the day.
Sorry, but there's nothing else to say, so
Don't ask me if you don't like what you get.
I love you. No, I don't. Again. Again.
The final yes or no has not come yet,
Until then all I do is re-explain
That "No, I don't." means no I don't—right now.
"I love you." means I love you—more or less.
I know it doesn't help things anyhow
To say that yes or no is just a guess,
But, since I don't feel any other way
Both yes and no is all I have to say.

Disorder

For yet another pill will stop the throb
And push of what we never want to think,
But must think, must think, must think. There's no job
Like obsession for the weary. No chink
In our mental armor is too small to
Become a gaping hole for worry and
For fret unless we take the pills, which do
Nothing in the long run, but make us stand
Our fears a bit better in the short, so...
Down the hatch they go, the prescription pills
That ease our anxious to-s and fro-s. We know
They don't cure what ever it is that kills
Our inner peace...but they settle the stress.
And, once we take them, we could not care less.

Quid Pro Quo

And what was I supposed to do? You took
Everything that ever made anything
Matter to me and then you tossed it, shook
It apart, and crushed it under. Nothing
Was left worth salvaging, let alone worth
Saving outright. You ruined my life. I
Was devastated. I couldn't go forth
From there. Neither should you. Imagine my
Chagrin to find you alive. Sorry that
You're not dead. I had no experience
With guns. I aimed too low and when I shot,
I missed your heart—although it's common sense
That a bullet paralyzing your spine
Should make you wish you were dead...which is fine.

Small Things

The cat food can's spilled fishy glop along
The counter where dirty dishes are stacked
Beside the sink. I'd put it down the wrong
Side up and juice trickled out while they snacked

(They being the cats) on salmon with sauce
Served in clean bowls. The irony doesn't
Escape me. Neither does the smell, a cross
Of old tuna, sea brine and redolent

Garbage. I ought to go and dump it in
The trash outside, but the weather's bad and I'm
Tired. I will live with it, one pet food tin
Won't kill me. Besides it's not that much time

Until morning when the dishes and the cat
Mess can be dealt with thoroughly. Now, I
Will shut the kitchen door...and that is that.
Always ways around small things if we try.

I'll Have Nothing, Thank You

I could never request a final dish
That would bring any sort of peace to me.
I have no dinner memories, no rich
Family suppers I loved. I grew up free
From pleasant associations with food.
We never ate French or Italian;
All our evening fare came ready-made: stewed,
Hashed, creamed…canned or boxed…Vulgarian
At best. Worse, living organisms died
To be thrown on dinner plates, slightly apart
From the sides (two, both flavorless). I've tried,
Honestly, but every time that I start
To think about which childhood meal would
Comfort me, I stop. Cold. None of them could.

And Again

So, now you're asking if I love you. Twice
Now, as a matter of fact. Oh God, I
Don't know if I love you or not. The nice
Times we've had so far were just that—nice. Why,
Pick them apart for meaning? That's not love,
That's measurement...looking for that something,
That slightly removed, that hidden start of
"Us"...which isn't there at all. You're playing
A game, nothing more. A win or lose, (no
Draw), gamble. With three words as the prize.
You obviously don't understand though,
That even if I say I love you, can a lie
Thusly regulated, matter? Of course
Not. It's just what I'll say to you...because.

Elegy for Portland, Oregon

Our grey skies are darker now with smoke borne
From Chinese factories out across the
Sea, blown by ocean breezes and the strong
Pacific winds we once extolled as a
Plus to living up here, where skies and seas
Tend to blur (by this I mean, of course, rains
And the deep wet damp that falls on to these
Portland streets we love). But, now we can't praise,
With old watery pride, our distinct lack
Of sun. We've lost the raw beauty of our
Dark rains to heavy metals; the smoke stacks
That belch blacker clouds than ours each hour
Have reached our damp hung sky. We are left
With dim haze...both polluted and bereft.

Work de Trop

*"The chief pleasure of rhyme is the rage
it inspires in its opponents."* —Paul Valéry

Do you think it matters? This poetry
We write in meter and submit until
This journal or that one accepts it. We
Don't have a hope in hell of being Will
Shakespeare or the new Percy Shelley, they're
All taken, those positions. And no one
Is looking to create new ones out there.
Face it, no-one wants what's considered "done":
Form's been anthologized, and left to rest,
Sanitized as old fashioned rhymes. Our new
Takes on that old game are de trop at best
And unwanted at large....Again, do you
Think it matters, this formal war we wage?
Let's hope so, if only just to enrage.

Once

The sink's full of gray water. Suds gone. Cold.
The handle of a pot, thrust in sideways,
Sticks out like a drowning man's arm. The old
Nickel faucet drips. Slowly, slowly...Rays
Of concentric circles emerge and fade,
Passing over things that limmer beneath
The surface. Coffee cups. Greasy bowls laid
One on top of the other. Forks like teeth
Standing tine side up in a mug. A vase
Whose rim just touches the top. Like a dot.
Or a circle drowned away. The sink was
White once. Empty once. But, 'once' isn't what
Gets dirty dishes done. 'Once' files away
A memory. Wet dishes sit for days.

Touché

Why bother to fight? My attention span
Only lasts three minutes, so you
Say. So, call it even, (though when it began
It was, like, 98 to two,
your favor. I always lose everything.
In the end, you know). Anyway,
Delete my emails, here's your cut price ring
There's not much left for me to say...
Except...I never really loved you. (Quite
The opposite in fact, you know,
You never really were my Mr. Right.
I just felt sorry for you). Now go.

I Despise You

I despise you, simply put. No more, no
Less. I think my life will be greatly—so
Greatly—enhanced when you've dropped dead that I
Find myself daydreaming of how you'll die.
A car crash, bone cancer, a glancing blow
To the temple by someone else I know
Who hates you as much as I do, merlot
And downers, a gunshot, a stabbing. Why?
I despise you.
You are a pig, a cow, a black widow,
A viper. Self-centered, self-serving, low
And grasping in mind and deed. A horsefly
Feeding on the sweat of others. I sigh
And think about you every day, although
I despise you.

What Isn't Burned Must Rot

What Isn't Burned Must Rot.

Skin shrivels on the bone, soft flesh dissolves.
Cells dry and crack, then break. Mildews encroach.
Nothing helps hold back decay. Form evolves.

Eons ago, our ancestors' approach
To this was simple: burn every body,
Old ashes do not stink or leak. But we—
Riddled as we are with deft morticians—
We do not do that anymore. We broach.
We pick. We buy our graves on time. We coach
Our families on our final plans. Heavens!
You'd think we thought that corpses somehow know.

Rains eat away the stone above the plot,
And if not rain, then wind, if not wind, snow.
Death is fact based: what isn't burned...must rot.

Branwell Bronte to His Sisters
on the occasion of his last illness

Don't hand me that old 'There there' lie.
I'm a failure. Spent. Done. Shot.
I haven't done the things that I
Swore I would. I'll die. I'll rot.
My name won't mean a damn at all.
My youthful boasts were just a joke.
I am a nothing. There there? What gall.
I die forgotten. Unknown. Broke.

And Again and Again and Again…

I don't know and there's the pain…
But we'll part and say goodbye
To what we had because we've found
That somehow something must've died
That somehow something's not around
That was.
        We'll never meet again.

Apostrophe To Death

You have no claim upon us; we're in love.
To die, hearts must falter, before they grow
Cold and feelingless. But our time above
The grave can't end: we are in love, and so
Our hearts shall never falter, we won't lie
Down dead. No, only loveless people die.

Does this bother you? Surely you've seen, Death,
Love like this before. Some dead heart still full
With it? Or maybe not? Perhaps our breadth,
Our span, our length of passion makes quite null
The common pulse of ardors belonging to
All others who have said their loves were true?

Touch yourself, Death. Our mortal fears of you
Are gone. We are more powerful than kings;
We are the grand architects of time, few
Before us have possessed such precious things:
Shared hearts, shared lips. Foul Death, you shall never
Come between us. Love's not made to sever.

At St. Alban's Churchyard

Old headstones—namelessly eroded—green
and grey with speckled moss in the sudden light
that fell after this morning's rain. The bright
sparkle of the sun reflected in between
these markers, where crevassed droplets fell
on webs, wet-laden now and spider-less.

So do our lives always come down to this:
damp stones in sunny boneyards. Nothing else.

Buttercups and Graves,
France 1921

Beneath the grey blue sky
Green trees and wild grass grow.
Buttercups multiply
And bees and sparrows fly
Where bees and sparrows go
Beneath the grey blue sky.

There's no real need to cry
While this graveyard can show
Buttercups multiply
As soon as people die
And shield them, head to toe
Beneath the grey blue sky.

Remember? You and I
Noticed amid our woe:
Buttercups multiply.
As years have gone on by
It's comforting to know:
Beneath the grey blue sky
Buttercups multiply.

Operation Freedom
(The Hammersmith Widow Speaks To the Grieving Mother)

Don't give me that old 'you'll meet again' bit
As you rearrange your son's photographs.
Because we can't. He's dead. I'm not. That's it.
I begged him not to go, and one bullet
Proved my worries right. I won't have your gaff.
Don't give me that old 'you'll meet again' bit—
As your son's smile fades away, post obit,
And graffiti litters the cenotaph—
Because we can't. He's dead. I'm not. That's it
For us. We're gone. He's him. I'm me. We're split
Apart by war and freedom's aftermath.
Don't give me that old 'you'll meet again' bit
Not one word. I won't listen. The casket
Might have come back—but not "us", not by half,
Because we can't: he's dead, I'm not. That's it,
There's no marriage left to us now. Visit
Some one else for your tears and flags, half-staff.
Don't give me that old 'you'll meet again' bit
Because we can't. He's dead. I'm not. That's it.

After the Colliery Collapse
A Sonnet in Torno Form

Where are the wreaths and bouquets? Huge masses
(There should be masses) of them, all heaped high--
Bloom on bloom on bloom? There's just grasses,
Tight cropped, trampled and intersected by
Gloom coloured scars that mark the edges where,
Despite the diggings, you were left unfound
Down there. To rot. To moulder. Left down there--
There where fifty of you worked too far down.
Found some of you, but not all. No. Despite
Where they thought you would be, it seems gloom,
By way of collapsed tunnels, held you tight.
Grasses grow here still, wild flowers will bloom
High and bright. Not that you'll know, though, you down there—
Masses of you—unknowing, unaware.

Ruined Cemetery

Violets no longer grow in the shaded places
Here and there among the thick Victorian stones
And the more recently enterred. There are no traces
That there ever were violets there. And these old bones
Won't tell you much, even if you should ask them to,
They can't. Their mouths were closed too many years ago,
They slumber now beneath some thorny weeds and a few
Dried out bits of yellow grass. Nothing much can grow
In here now; they do not water, nor do they prune.
It's all a tangled mess of burr covered stems—long
Busy with the task of wearing down the graves. Soon
There will be nothing here to see but them. It's wrong
Perhaps, of me to care so much, my bones don't lay
Beneath rough weeds. But, part of me still knows: they may.

Winter Stand

Autumn comes with cold rain. Wet leaves pillow
The ground as spattered droplets fall, tantrum-
Like and loud, drumming the town with silver
Splashes that fall upon these woods and my roof.
My neighbors will leave here soon. They'll succumb
To the fears of inevitable snow

That winters here bring. My neighbors say snow
Fall around here's too high, they fear pillow
On pillow of drifts: no break...Bah! Succumb
To those fears and nature's autumn tantrum
Can begin to magnify itself. Roof
And wall can seem not enough. Silver

And gold can seem not enough: Gold? Silver?
They can't fix what winter could wring with snow,
With cold, with ice. I don't care, though. My roof
Is sound, my walls are thick. Let drifts pillow
The fields and the hills. I'll have no tantrum,
No sudden urge to flee while I succumb

To fears like my neighbors', or to succumb
To their ways: dry southern heat and silver
Sanded beaches each winter, where tantrum-
Dark skies cannot occur...No, let it snow
Until I cannot leave, until pillow
After pillow is piled up to my roof,

Erasing all outward escape. The roof
Will creak, and the walls...but, they won't succumb,
Won't buckle. They've stood it so far. Pillow
It on! Pile it against this place. Silver
My windows and my ledges with ice. Snow

Cannot win against my house, no tantrum

Of weather can un-snug me here. Tantrum,
Deluge, storm, I'll stay here, under my roof.
And, unlike those who flee before the snow,
I'll have the time to watch the world succumb
To autumn's urgings, and, as the silver
Icy time of winter and snow's pillow

Comes, with a soft pillow myself, tantrum-
Free and silver haired, I'll sleep while my roof
Does not succumb to any weight of snow.

Because

And so we come across the end. I knew
It was about to come: the signs we saw
(Make no mistake, love, they were there, but you
Thought that they would look different, because
You just assumed they would), the way things felt
Between us these last few years (maybe I
Should add: the way things didn't feel too. No melt,
No burn, nothing at all but distance). Try
As I might, I can't pretend (the way that
You pretend) that I couldn't tell, that we
Were blindsided by this sudden dead flat
Place we've found ourselves in. Oh, we could see
What was happening alright, both of us
Could. But, you didn't believe it. Because.

To A Long Dead Friend

Thanks. I don't know if you can hear people
Where you're at, or if you want to, being
As you've been gone from here for years. But still...
I hope you can, because I've been feeling
That there is some thing that I want to tell you,
About how much having you around meant
To me, and how much I miss you. But who
Knows how to speak to the dead? We repent,
We confess, we pray, we supplicate. We
Don't talk to our dead friends, though, anymore,
So I might be going about this pretty
Much the wrong way, at least style-wise, or
Perhaps it makes no difference? If so,
Well, then, thanks. I just wanted you to know.

After
Regarding The Little Mermaid

*"...it is by no means certain that the ending is
as happy as it seems to be"*
—Jacob Bøggild & Pernille Heegaard

Now that I am turned foam, I cannot search
The bright Atlantic stars that mark the sky
Across his world and back again, for I
Can not see anything now. Wide waves lurch
And throw me back and forth; the thrashing sea
Is green with my new self. I can not find
Those daughters of the air who were so kind
To me. The deep water pushes at me
Until long ropes of reaching sea weeds curl
And drag me under...pulling...pulling...deep.
Deep down I go, to where the ocean keeps
Sunken things far from prince's mortal worlds.
I lay waterlogged and lost; no star
Will ever shine its brilliance down this far.

Don't Come Around

Don't come around. I don't need
Witnesses to watch me bleed
My dignity and dreams and away—
To tell me that ideals don't pay—
To settle on my veins and feed—
To smear all my life's work and say:
We never liked you anyway.

Respice Finem

A thin wooden fence, runs—fallen in and
Rotted—with splintered pieces scattered on
Broken stones, and weeds. Two upright posts stand
In derelict attention as if they,
In this manner, can somehow countermand
The horror of neglect and long decay.

Loved ones were left here, to mould and decay
Beneath headstones carved with names and dates and
Information designed to countermand
The loss of who they were when they passed on,
(The loss of every single thing that they
Were and did). Now the old stones—broken—stand

Mutely for those who may no longer stand.
Those who were left to rankle and decay
By persons, loved ones more alive than they,
Who buried them here, to slumber on and
Then left them here as the years rolled on.
And nothing can be done to countermand

The harsh toll of years. Try to countermand
As much as you wish, the effects still stand—
Nothing can be done to roll back time. On
It rolls, onward to the end and to decay,
Onward to the loss of everything. And
We shall, ourselves, be as lost. Just as they

Are left, in this neglected place, as they
Are left without a hope of countermand
To stem the process, we will be left. And
Surely we too shall come to understand
The erasure of ourselves. Deft decay

Will leave little of us to carry on
The same way there is little of them. On
Ward goes time and onward go we. As they
Are now, so we will also be. Decay
Councils no brook, no stop, no countermand.
No matter how strong our own headstones stand
One day they will break, taking the names and

Dates carved on them. Despite the countermand
That they must last they will not always stand
Above us and outlast the last decay.

To Be or Not To Be

And what difference does it make anyway
being as nothing here is permanent or
closed to further circumstances. Things here
arise, then fall...or do not rise always
at all. But it makes no difference, for
time moves, death comes. Year by year by year.

Yet we struggle through our lives somehow
pretending, frantically, that we have no fear,
and no real regret that we will last no more
than the brief flaring moment we're each allowed
To appear.

Sparrows in January

Sparrows In January

Sparrows flit and peck the freezing
Snow while blue shadows from the trees
Fall across the whiteness, pleasing
Poets and artists, but not these
Small birds. It's cold here, the winter's
Been hard, and long, icy splinters
Of hail and chilling heaps of snow
Have all given the sparrows no
Break, only cold icy mornings
Bringing cold icy days. Who
Has not seen the tiny things through
A window, (while news warnings
Advise we stay indoors and warm),
Searching for cold crumbs in a storm?

Sonnenizio with Keat's Blue Sonnet

Blue! Tis the life of heaven—the domain
Of everything that's glorious: the air,
The sea, the far flung domain where our gods
Entered our world from heaven, and remain
—Some of them—here for life. Devils may care
For scarlet, tis said—to hell with that. Clods
Claim brown (who needs it). Green's the domain of
Fairy life—the sage stems of it belong
To them and them alone. Gold's the life hue
Of the wise ones, of bright sunshine, of love,
And of patience...but blue! Blue is birdsong
From the domain of air at mid day. Blue
Is life's highest holiness, a shadow-
Glimpse of heaven itself, down here, below.

Nearly Still Life, Shire Morning

Furling—and then uncurling—thin smoke slides
in lazy spirals which moor the morning
as it dashes up from night. Breezes cross,
re-arranging greyness along the yard
where it mingles with fruit blossoms. Inside
the brightly lit cottages the dawn brings
great thoughts of bacon, toast, brimming tea pots.
White sunshine pulses out from behind red-
tinged hills that touched the edge of dawn. Hens scratch
and take their cackles to the shire's trees
where smoke has trailed and petals head ground-ward,
soft falling—grey and pink—until they catch
the brisk currents of the new morning's breeze
and dance, swirling, in perfect disregard.

January Woods

Grey barked and silent, each slumbering tree
Waits—a hushed sentinel—for coming spring,
Warmth and longer days. These bleakest wintry
Months offer only frozen days which bring
Nothing to sap, or to root, that can be
Good. So the trees sleep on while snow flakes fling

From leaden skies to land on bare limbs, fling
Down on last year's leaves, fling down on each tree,
Each piece of root, keeping all that may be
Frozen, frozen firmly until the spring.
There is nothing that the cold may do or bring
Which will wake these sleepers from their wintry

Rest. They grasp the chilly dirt in wintry
Embrace, cold roots fixed firmly, while clouds fling
Ice-hail-snow and chilly winter winds bring
Storms that howl and rattle through every tree—
Whipping leafless branches as if a spring
Were pushed against itself and then let be,

Lashing and tossing through the trees, to be-
Come a roaring, thrashing force: the wintry
Soul of nature. While woods dream of spring
Dream of warm breezes, of blossoms that fling
From ends of twigs and set alight each tree
With fragrance and life and colors that bring

The robins that twitter branch to branch, bring
The bright winged harbinger of life: the bee
Whose pleasant drone grows loud within the tree
As it stops in every bloom. Those wintry

Dreams are rooted, deep, far from where skies fling
Down snow...snow which seems to forever spring

From heavy clouds. The trees wait for the spring
To finally come. They wait for it to bring
Them warmth and light and fine showers that fling
Themselves into puddles. They wait to be
Free of frost and chilly winds, of wintry
Rains that freeze. Patiently, patiently, tree

After tree waits for Spring, waiting to be
Woken when the days bring no more wintry
Tree-freezing gales...just sun-warmed rains that fling.

Disting Fae

There are no leaves left within these winter
branches—just twigs and sticks that complicate
the sky with stark crossings and sharp inter-
crossings against a backdrop of tin-plate
coloured clouds. Snow flakes, sifting through the maze
made by these greenless trees, freeze on, and cloak
each naked branch. Instead of leaves, cold glaze
smoothly hugs these chilly woods. Oak
maple, elm: how still they are, with icy
gloves on all their frozen tips. And then, from
out of nowhere, landing improbably
in the winter trees, small wing'ed things come,
one after another, laughing as they
wake the snowy branches, then fly away.

Vogelblut

A line of scarlet spots in well trimmed grass:
Stark and sudden, it consumes the light. Red
Heightened by sunrays and a virent mass
Of thin leaves. Red that seems to have been bled
From the mind's eye, the colour pure and right—
No orange there, no blue to bring to mind
Other shades, other objects. These lined bright
Circles are all the same, only one kind
Of red drops like that upon a lawn. Blood.
It can't be anything else but blood here
Where there are no paints, no rubies, no floods
Of pomegranate juice. Just birds, which veer
Too close to household cats, and so are caught—
Leaving small drops to drape each emerald stalk.

The Grove in Shade and Light

The Grove in Shade and Light

Leaves dance and shafts of sunlight flicker down
Between them. Shadows—made from shifting sun
While swaying branches move and swing around—
Grow thick and dark upon each patch of ground
Beneath them, then are suddenly undone.
Leaves dance and shafts of sunlight flicker down
The same no matter that the shadows found
One minute are dissolved the next. Begun
While swaying branches move and swing around,
The shadows swell and pool and then are drowned
By light, cascading, while in unison
Leaves dance and shafts of sunlight flicker down
Some more, and new shades form in new surrounds
Of branches under shifting trees. Each one,
While swaying branches move and swing around,
A blur of motion and of shade. Each crowned
With bright green brilliance: halcyon
Leaves dance…and shafts of sunlight flicker down
While swaying branches move and swing around.

The Sacred Spiral

I know little how a season turns, why
Cold winds slowly change to warm, when the rain
Will fall or else hang darkly in the sky
Waiting, waiting, within a counterpane
Of thick grey cloud. I cannot tell why leaves
Grow dull and thin and fall away, or what
Sleeping spirit lurks in the cold bare trees
That wakens and makes new greenery. Hot
Days and cold, and warm lazy afternoons--
Each holds a magic apart from what I
Will ever know. But does it matter? June
Will surely come and then become July,
And fade away into the fall and then
To winter...spring...and back to June again.

Winter's Night, Farm Fields, Old Burton on Trent

Overhead, clouds that sat sky-spread and ashy white
are dim edged now and grey. Long shadows point their black
fingers down across the leafless trees. Mosses, light
green against the blackness, turn black themselves as night
lends its somber covering to all. A faint track
of stars – half obscured by the glut of grey edged clouds
that hang thick against the setting sun—dimly steals
across the darkening sky, making darker still
this break with day. Fog, slipping from the soil, enshrouds
and funnels down between the shadowed trees until
it whips away to drape with darkness far off hills
that mark the furthest corners of these ancient fields.

Spring Softly Comes
Sondeau*

Spring softly comes with little hints of green
Set vividly on brown bare branches, seen
As emerald leaf tips in garden rows, bright
And brilliant against the stark black and white
Bleakness that was winter. There's a serene
Majesty in this turn around, a keen
Sense of life fulfilled and fulfilling, been
And becoming. Needing no one's invite
Spring softly comes.
On breezes that it brings itself with clean
Clear days of cloudless skies, set between
Warm evenings that give in to delight
A little more with each successive night
Spring softly comes.

a sonnet/rondeau

Late Spring

Across the green new grass that grows upon the brown
Where seed has not yet sprung, the petals slowly fall
In airy patterns—fashioned by an early breeze—
Of random whorls and hinted spirals on the ground.
One might expect to simply stand and see them all
Drop down in mute agreement from the laden trees.

The whole orchard yard itself grows pale with these:
White blossoms blown across themselves and down
To end in tumbled heaps against the garden wall.

Late April Storm

Damp flowers drop from ever damper trees
so all along the grass and ground there are
small wet petals strewn about. Each of these
blown down and then washed out across the yard
by a late spring shower that was not meant
to come. But came despite it all, to show
that nature is always irreverent...
...no matter what we humans think we know.

Winter Clouds: Liverpool

Behind the jagged winter trees, the clouds—
Grey clad and thickly edgeless—merge and form
A vast dim dome with no relief at all;
Just sky gone ashy white and blank. A shroud
If you will, a winding sheet that holds storm
And keeps back the light until cold drops fall

Beneath and coat the branches as they fall
With ice that does not sparkle under clouds
That allow no light, allow no shine. Storm
And wind and cold may descend—any form
Of dark and dismalness within this shroud
May come, but nothing shiny...light...at all

Lies here these days. None may be seen at all
Of brightened mornings or afternoons that fall
Into brightened twilights. For this dull shroud,
This thick mantle of unremitting clouds,
Shuts away the world from every thing: form,
Beauty, light, all is gone from here. High storm

And denser gloom, then another high storm
That brings more gloom, have filled the season. All
The sky is filled with them; their lack of form
Creates a backdrop to grey days that fall
With no substance to them beneath the clouds
That cover everything. The swollen shroud

That smothers the light, the smothering shroud
That both comes after and foretells of storm,
Looms and glooms above us through these days. Clouds
Touching clouds, stretched out across the sky, all
Thickly spread and set with dull rains that fall

Without relief and within a formless form—

Even harder rains cannot break this form
Of ill-formed grey blankness, seamless grey shroud.
Rains fall, but nothing changes as they fall
Rains storm, but nothing alters as they storm.
The clouds remain, endlessly, after all.
Clouds upon clouds remaining as if clouds

Were one form of endless form. Hail, snow, storm,
Wind: nothing shifts the shroud that covers all
As cold dim days fall…beneath this dome of clouds.

Unhappy Wisdom

And to avoid the path to hell
We had to bid a fond farewell
To things well loved, now left behind.
We could not keep them.
                         They remind.

About Juleigh Howard-Hobson

About Juleigh Howard-Hobson

Born in England in 1963, Juleigh Howard-Hobson is primarily a formalist poet, but she has also written literary fiction, genre work, and non-fiction essays and articles. Like W. B. Yeats she walks a line between this world and that other, sometimes un-seen, world.

Her poems have been published in many journals, including Trinacria, The Lyric, The New Formalist, The Hypertexts, The Pennsylvania Review, Hex Magazine, The Raintown Review, Mezzo Cammin, Umbrella, Qarrtsiluni, 14 by 14, Caduceus: The Poets at Art Place, vol. 8 (Yale University), North American New Right (Counter Currents), The Best of the Barefoot Muse (Barefoot Muse) and Poem, Revised: 54 Poems, Re-visions, Discussions (Marion Street Press).

Her books include Sommer & Other Poems and The Cycle of Nine, both with RavensHalla Arts Publications, as well as I Don't Belong to the Baader Meinhof Group & Other Poems (Counter Currents). She also edited The Runestone Journal, vol. 1 (AFA/RavensHalla).

Her work has been nominated for both "The Best of the Net" and The Pushcart Prize.

A mother of three, she lives a radical traditionalist life on a micro-farm in the Pacific Northwest.

www.ingramcontent.com/pod-product-compliance
Lightning Source LLC
Chambersburg PA
CBHW070532100426
42743CB00010B/2050